ISBN: 9781736175903

CHRISTMAS GIFT SERIES

Good Gift Books

and Merchandise™

From the Editor

The odds are very good that you've never received a Christmas card like this before. It includes a verse that's very similar to those you might have read in traditional Christmas cards, but it is filled with far too much Christmas Spirit to be kept to a couple pages. Instead, this card is spread out over the length of a full book. But, that's not the most exciting part about the card you're currently holding: This text allows you to decide the direction the verse will take.

This book isn't intended to be read straight through. There are prompts throughout the text giving you options for what direction you would like the verse to take. You might get the gist if you read it linearly, but that might take all of the fun out of it.

We hope you enjoy this journey, and that you and yours have a wonderful holiday season.

Merry Christmas!

Violet Jade

Christmas Verse Just Ahead!

You've never
received a
Christmas card
like this before ...

Most cards just
have two pages,
or, at best,
there's four.

This card has more Christmas spirit than the ones sold at the store ...

So the person
who gave you
this card
clearly loves
you more!

This card puts you
in the driver's seat,
and lets you pick
its tone ...

You choose where to go next, so you can make it all your own.

Just flip to
your desired
page when
the prompts
appear ...

And allow the
words to fill
you with joyous
Christmas
cheer.

Here's how it works:
Begin this journey
by choosing the
overall direction
of this Christmas
verse:

*Nostaligic & Happy
(Go to Page **44**)

or

*Sincere & Sappy
(Go to Page **54**)

look back, where
DON'T plot
revenge

This is a pleasant
look back, where
I DON'T plot

revenge ...

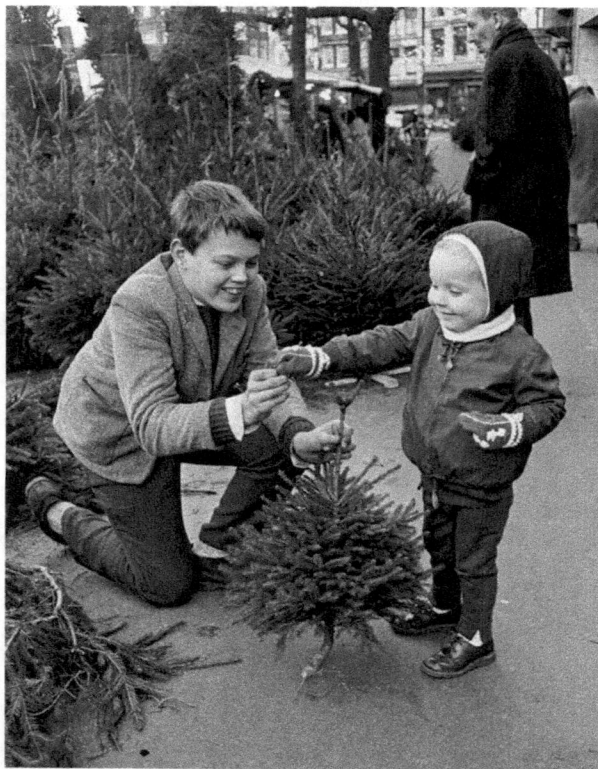

On those who
snapped holiday
pictures that now just
make me cringe.

Of traditions
we'd keep ...

and traditions
we'd make ...

We'd gather around trees, some of which weren't even fake.

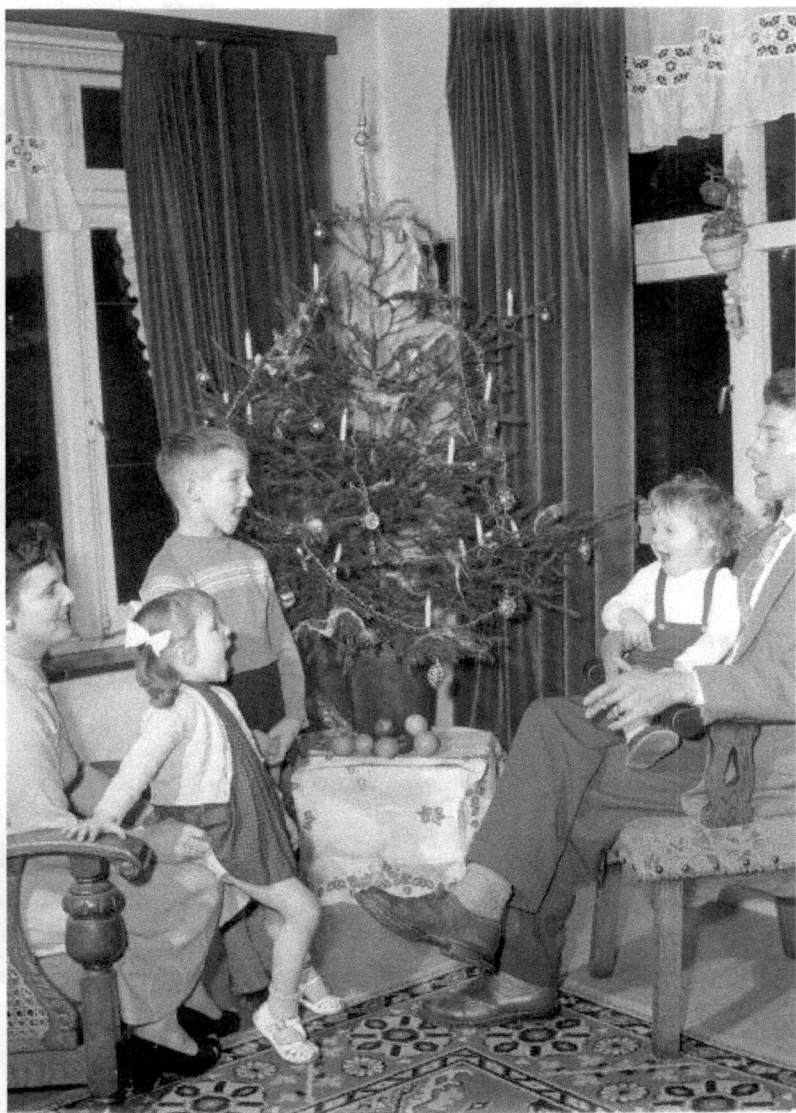

We did so many tasks,
but none felt like
"work" ...

We'd open our presents,
and then go berserk.

Christmas gift shopping didn't make me want to get into fights ...

I never thought
of electric bills
when I saw
festive lights.

*To reflect a little on what
Christmas means,
Go to Page **64**.

or

*To revisit some Christmas
memories,
Go to Page **80**.

Learning that it feels
as good to give as it
does to receive ...

We carry on
traditions on the big
day and its Eve.

From the burdens
we have in life, this
day is a reprieve ...

We find ourselves
wishing we never
had to leave.

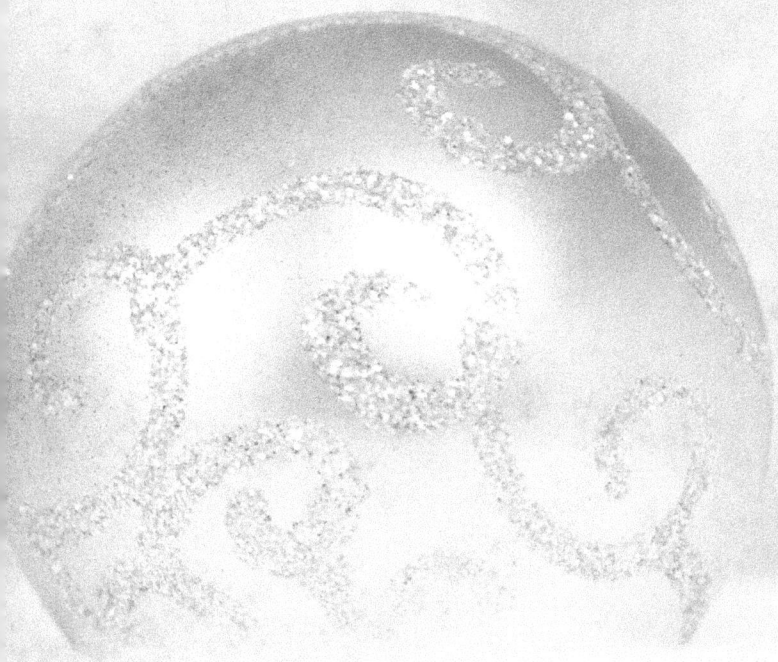

We look at photos
of good times from
bygone years ...

Warmth rushes
our hearts, and
our eyes fill with
tears.

Memories feel close as
joyous music fills
our ears ...

Rekindling the
excitement felt when
we knew Santa's
sleigh nears.

*To reflect a little on
what Christmas means,
Go to Page **64**.

or

*To revisit some
Christmas memories,
Go to Page **80**.

As I take a
look back ...
Reflect ...
Remember ...

On events that transpired 'round the 25th of December ...

The Christmas of
old just seemed
to be best ...

But today,
Christmas often
makes me just
want to rest.

It's fun to think
back at how
things once
were ...

When we weren't
quite so hussled
and it wasn't all
just a blur.

But how, if I'm
feeling like I
just can't
take it ...

I remind myself
simply:
Christmas IS what
we make it.

*If you want the verse to
take a funny turn,
Go to Page **20**

or

*To reflect a little on what
Christmas means,
Go to Page **64**.

Christmas is the
coziest time of
the year ...

When cold
weather pivots
to brings us all
cheer.

Not just with
hot chocolate
and ginger
beer ...

But with warmth
from the people
whom we hold
most dear.

Reflecting on
old times and
how they made
us feel ...

Or gathering
with loved ones,
to share a cozy
meal.

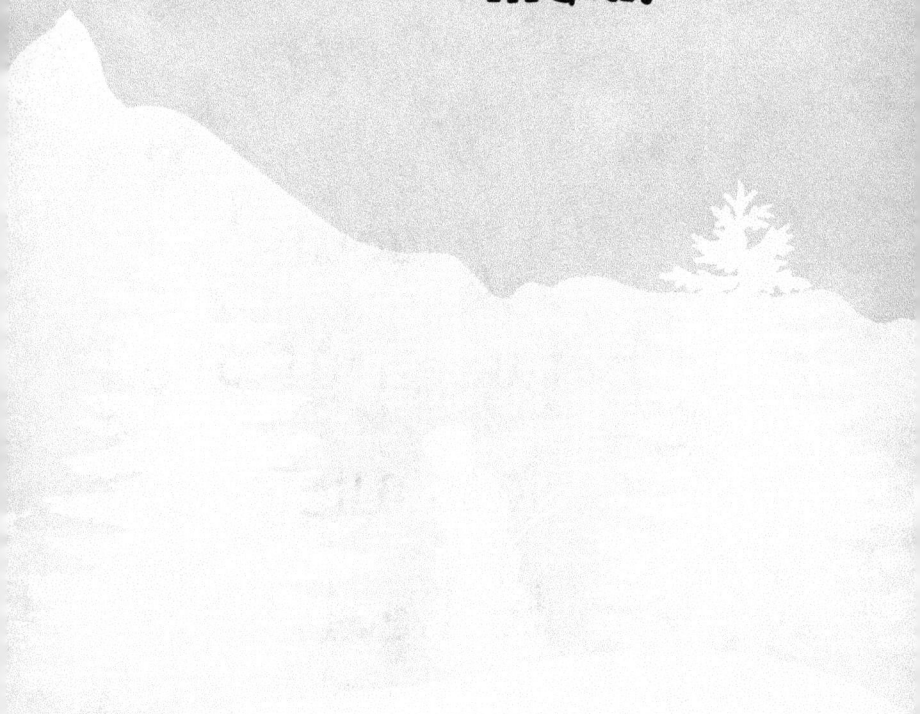

Any wounds
between us are
at last allowed
to heal ...

Frozen hearts
always melt when
we focus on what's
real.

*To revisit some Christmas
memories,
Go to Page **80**.

or

*If you want the verse to
get warm and fuzzy,
Go to Page **34**.

Singing songs
that stir our
hearts like they
did long, long
ago ...

Carols that are
so much a part of
us, even babies
seem to know.

We radiate so much cheer, as if we were never feeling low ...

We fill up with so
much love, as if
we've never had
a foe.

Watching movies we
first saw when we
could only crawl ...

Singing songs we first
learned when we
were two feet tall.

Soaking
up what's
happening,
details big and
small ...

Creating memories
our future selves
will joyously
recall.

It's like the
feeling on a cold
day beneath a
fluffy cover ...

A day that brings
us together much
more than any
other.

Forgetting our
differences and
treating strangers
like a brother ...

Reflecting on what
matters most:
Loving one another.

***Turn to Page 96 to read
the final verse**

Back in the day,
a Christmas that
was simple, didn't
seem lame ...

No mind if every
Santa Claus didn't
look the same.

We would pray
for snow with all
of our might ...

But get over
it fast if the
weather wasn't
just right.

What presents we'd get, held us all in suspense ...

And not a single thought wasted on current events.

If things went
wrong it never
seemed tragic ...

The air itself felt
just a little bit
magic.

As each year creeps
toward Christmas,
and we all prepare ...

I think back to past
Christmases, and
inevitably declare:

I'm sure things
weren't exactly as
I remember ...

When I look back on the 25th of December.

Things might not have
been that simple,
but this is
no documentary.

For the Christmases
are perfect as is —
stored in my memory.

**Turn to Page 96 to read
the final verse.**

Whether you prefer sappy, funny, happy, or sincere ...

Christmas is,
in fact, the
greatest time
of year.

Where we can
spend time with
those we hold
dear ...

And fill each
other's lives,
and hearts,
with cheer.

This card is
unlike any
you've ever
had ...

Filled with choices, none of them bad.

You have picked
your path on your
own ...

And with each
turn you've set
the tone.

It's our
deepest wish
right from the
start ...

That Christmas
spirit will fill your
heart ...

And for joy in
your life to always

increase ...

For your world
to be filled with
endless peace.

We wish you
and yours
a very
Merry
Christmas!

We hope you've

enjoyed your copy of

"Self-Guided Christmas Card."

Hopefully this book has helped

enhance your Christmas spirit

and the love between you and

the special people in your life.

Good Gift Books
and Merchandise™

If you liked this book, you might like something else in Good Gift Books' Book-Length Greeting Card series. Available on Amazon.

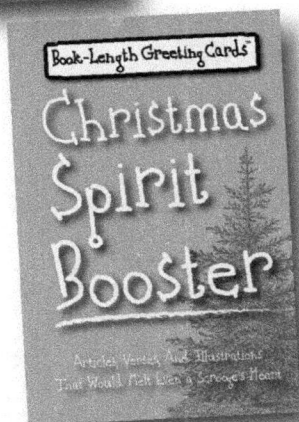

Book-Length Greeting Cards

I wish you a _____ Christmas

A Fill-in-the-blank Christmas Verse for a Personalized Holiday Message

Book-Length Greeting Cards

Self-Guided Christmas Card

A nostalgic holiday verse that lets readers plot their own path

Book-Length Greeting Cards

Christmas Spirit Booster

Articles, Verses, And Illustrations That Would Melt Even a Scrooge's Heart

www.ingramcontent.com/pod-product-compliance
Lightning Source LLC
Chambersburg PA
CBHW060510280326
41933CB00014B/2906